MAKING MONEY WHILE YOU SLEEP

SELLING ON AMAZON UK & THE REST OF EUROPE

BY JASON A. KWAO

Dedication

I dedicate this book to my partner in life, business, and success, my fiancée, who has always given me more than I bargained for. Also, my beautiful daughter, who has given me an incredible zest for life and reminded me of what it feels like to be a child again.

To my family and friends, I appreciate all the love and support, and I pray you to live long, prosperous lives.

Preface

Thank you for purchasing this book. I put my best foot forward in making sure you get the most value out of your purchase. If you like this book, make sure you leave a review, and if you have any suggestions for improvement, please send us an email at jaxs-education@outlook.com.

Why did I decide to write this book?

My passion for writing this book came from a place of wanting to help people succeed in their financial life. Going through struggles myself and not being able to find a way to prosperity, I promised myself I would help anyone willing to learn once I found a method.

After one year and six months of selling on Amazon, I've been able to retire at the young age of 23, enjoying precious moments with my newborn daughter. I believe this is achievable for anyone and can be done within six months to one year if you follow the principles within this book.

How did I start selling on Amazon?

After a lengthy battle of being stuck between continuing my studies at university and wanting to create financial freedom, I dropped out of university to pursue my dream of making money online. It wasn't all sunshine and roses I can tell you that. It was a risk and looking back; I'm surprised my fiancée, then having been my girlfriend for only a month, supported my decisions, which I'll always love her for.

I had no job, no income, solely a gigantic goal, and a dream of one day reaching it. During this time, I worked a few odd jobs and gained a substantial amount of money, which I constantly reinvested, seeking higher return rates. Some of my prior investments were peer to peer lending and investing in index funds.

After considering what my next move was going to be, I remember watching a video on selling on Amazon FBA (Fulfilled by Amazon) and started digging deeper into it. I had a few losses, some small, some large, but on your journey to financial freedom, you will fail. That is guaranteed. But it's up to you to decide what you do after failing. You either give up or get back up. This leads perfectly into my favourite quote by Napoleon Hill, author of Think & Grow Rich.

"Every adversity, every failure, every heartache carries with it the seed of an equal or greater benefit" - **Napoleon Hill.**

Welcome on your journey to financial freedom and abundance. I hope to meet you soon and hear your story too!   *Jason A. Kwao Birmingham,2020*

Introduction

Money. What type of emotions comes up for you when you hear that word? No! Really stop and think about how you feel. For me, it's freedom, time, peace, and prosperity. For others, it may be fear, being in debt, or thinking about bills. But whatever the situation may be, money is something we all have to deal with. It might not be as important as oxygen, but it's definitely up there somewhere.

So if money is so important, why are we taught so little about it? Is it because the rich want to stay rich, or because the rich need the poor to stay poor? I can't give you a definite answer, but surely there must be a reason for it all. Luckily some millionaires have been generous enough to share their knowledge and experience of creating wealth. I've read most of the literature, applied a lot of the theories, and experienced failure several times, so you don't have to. Here, I'll be giving you the shortcut to success.

Even though the title says you can make money in your sleep, this is not a get-rich-quick scheme. It will require focus, patience, as well as diligence to stick with the journey. After this, you would have earned the luxury of making money in your sleep. Even though you might not get-rich-quick, this could be the fastest way for you to get rich. It certainly beats working a 9-5 job, putting your money in a retirement account, and trusting other people to manage your wealth. It is time to put the power back into your own hands and become your own boss!

To make sure you get the most value out of this book, I have included a few chapters which discuss ideas that will help you towards the creation of your wealth, especially if you are a beginner. Therefore, if you are only interested in creating an Amazon FBA business and you aren't interested in the wealth fundamentals, by all means, you can skip those chapters.

I would recommend you read this book thoroughly the first time and take notes/highlight as not to miss any important information. After you have a brief overview of the process, you can use it as a guide to help you through your journey.

Thank you, and I hope you enjoy the book.

Book Links

This book was initially designed for Kindle, therefore some of the images may not be as clear and links may not work as intended.

However I've created a URL which you can use to access all the included links and images: http://bit.ly/Pictureslinks

Table of Contents

The Winners Mindset

Traits needed to succeed in any endeavour

While building wealth, I used to believe I needed to develop only one skill in order for me to become successful. After years of searching, learning, and practising, I realised one skill simply wouldn't cut it. I needed to master a handful of skills to become wealthy.

It was until I studied the work of T. Harv Eker, author of the book 'Secrets of the Millionaire Mind.' Notice how I said 'studied' instead of 'read.' There is a slight but massive difference between these two words. When I decided to take the author up on his challenge to read the book once a month for a year, I started to notice things I had missed out before and ponder thoughts I had never considered before. I recommend both the book and the seminar, called the 'Millionaire Mind Intensive' to anyone serious about creating wealth, and if you're reading this book, I already know you're on the right track.

Having now experienced the power of committing myself to study T. Harv Eker's book, I discovered the mind is the first step for creating wealth. Your mindset will determine whether you will take the necessary actions for you to live the life of your dreams.

1. <u>Mindset </u>is so powerful that in my opinion, 80% of your success is determined by your mindset, whereas your skillset accounts for only 20%.

Imagine being a bodybuilder. You've got the physique, you train several times a week, and you know all the ins and out of weight lifting. You've got the skills down to a T. Now competition day comes, and you feel afraid, you're scared you might fail and risk humiliation. I'm sure we can all relate to the fear of failure. Comparatively, there's an amateur that's ambitious beyond belief and has a vision of what he could be. Being inspired by other champions, he decides to take a chance and sign up for the competition, even though he might fail and get laughed at, it drives his ambition. He learns all the skills he lacked initially, trains consistently, and eventually becomes the champion he always knew he would be.

2. <u>Persistence </u>is, according to the Oxford dictionary, the fact of continuing in an opinion or course of action in spite of difficulty or opposition.

Once you've got your mindset fixed, you will become focused on growing and becoming the person you know you can be. You are going to face some opposition. Scrap that, you'll face a lot of opposition. This could be from friends, family, partners, and even strangers who know nothing about you. But that is fine, nothing worth having comes easily.

When I decided to go on my entrepreneurial journey, I fell in love with the quote I stated previously from Napoleon Hill. I realised every adversity does bring with it an equal or greater benefit, and I will explain why.

While searching for my first product (which took me about three months due to inexperience), I found a product I believed to be great, but while discussing the financials with the supplier, I realised their prices were so high I wouldn't be able to turn a profit. After this setback, I immediately decided to get back on my horse and discovered a software called Jungle Scout. Using this software, I found my best-selling product just within a week of doing research, and I haven't looked back since.

3. "Formal education will make you a living; self-education will make you a fortune." - Jim Rohn

If you know me, you'll know I've always got a selection of audiobooks that I shamelessly share with anyone I come into contact with. Most of us already know that our formal education does not prepare us for the world outside of school. Skills including managing money, dealing with mental health, learning from failure, and many more are neglected.

Luckily for us, we've got access to the most incredible minds that have walked the face of this planet. We have the ability to pick the brains of business tycoons such as Andrew Carnegie and John Rockefeller, and investors like Warren Buffet and Ray Dalio, all through the nuggets they left behind in books.

The first book I read outside my formal education was a popular book that featured on Oprah called 'Rich Dad, Poor Dad' by Robert Kiyosaki. This book expanded my awareness of what was possible in the financial world—discussing ideas like the difference between an asset and a liability, how the rich don't work for money, and how they always mind their own business.

Having a clear vision

One of my favourite questions I like to ask people is, "Where do you want to be in 10 years?" Why? When people answer this question, it gives you an idea of what they think about on a day to day basis. And what you do, think, and act on today will determine where you will be tomorrow.

I remember when I was younger, around the age of 14, I used to wake up day to day, not knowing what was going to happen that day, week, or even year. I was drifting through life, as many people still do. Now fast-forward a few years, I've manifested many of my dreams, created several vision boards, and ticked off many goals I have set for myself.

As I was writing this book, the universe inspired me with a video on Youtube that discussed this exact principle—being in control of your life and your destiny by focusing on the daily decisions you make. In order to achieve the success that you want, you have to become a person who is capable of dealing with that success. Be - Do - Have. You have to become the person through your thoughts. You take action on those thoughts, and then, you will have the results you want.

If you're only starting your entrepreneurial journey now and you aren't yet sure of what you want from your life, you can start by creating a vision board. The definition of a vision board from the Oxford Dictionary is "a collage of images and words representing a person's wishes or goals, intended to serve as inspiration or motivation." Think about the people you look up to and inspire you. Think about the traits they possess, the lifestyle they live and think about what you want your life to be like in three, five, ten, twenty-five, and fifty years in the future.

"Most people overestimate what they can do in one year and underestimate what they can do in ten years." - Bill Gates

Imagine what you can do in a lifetime. Remember, no vision is too big!

The Case for Selling Online

E-commerce

During the last few decades, we've noticed a shift in how businesses operate in the economy. GOV.UK reported that in 2019, there were 19.2% of total retail sales placed online. This is an increase from 7.3% in 2010. The e-commerce space has been steadily growing and has seen a significant increase in 2020 due to the outbreak of COVID-19, which has forced a majority of brick and mortar businesses to shut down.

The World Retail Congress has also cited the UK as the 3rd top market for e-commerce, only being beaten by the USA for the 1st place and China for the 2nd. Despite this, the UK has 80% of the population shopping online, with total revenue of £77.83 billion. The market is mostly driven by millennials who are looking for a bargain, as well as fast shipping and free returns while browsing the web on their mobile phones.

With this in mind, it is no surprise that businesses are all rushing to grab a piece of the cake. As the market place is still relatively new and only accounting for 19.2% of sales in retail, there is still a huge slice left on the table for the best players.

Luckily for us, companies have made it easier for entrepreneurs like you and me to contribute to the growth in the economy. Setting up a website has never been easier using platforms like Wix, Shopify, and GoDaddy. Learning the skills to start your online business is accessible through platforms such as

Udemy, Kindle, and Skillshare. You can connect with likeminded people simply by having a quick search on Facebook or Twitter. So let's now get into the real reason why you're reading this book. Amazon.

Amazon

If you've shopped online, chances are you've bought from the e-commerce giant Amazon. Having started in 1994 during the dot-com boom, they initially focused on selling books, and have now expanded into areas such as artificial intelligence, cloud computing, and digital streaming. Amazon is now considered one of the big four tech companies, along with Google, Apple, and Microsoft. As of the 10th of July 2020, Amazon is worth a whopping $1.6 trillion.

With Amazon always keeping customers at the forefront of every decision and allowing sellers to leverage the platform, it's trillion-dollar valuation is well-earned. Sellers have the ability to sell from home or their warehouse, as well as also having the option of using Amazon's FBA service. Customers are able to receive their products on the same day or the next day by registering as Prime members. Other benefits of being a Prime member include streaming Amazon Prime Video, Prime Reading, exclusive discounts/savings, and more.

As Amazon continues to grow, there will be more opportunities for its sellers and creatives. Take, for example, the launch of the Kindle. Books are now available for buyers at a lower price and can easily be published and distributed through this format. Audiobooks are currently going through a similar opportunity where authors can pay for someone to narrate their book.

Amazon is currently the largest online marketplace serving countries worldwide. It has dedicated marketplaces for the United States, the United Kingdom, France, Ireland, Canada, Germany, Spain, Italy, Australia, Japan, China, India, Mexico, and many more with new marketplaces frequently being added. As we will be discussing how to start an FBA business within the UK, we will also discuss how you can sell and expand in the European marketplaces as well. This is either through the Pan-European Fulfilment by Amazon (Pan-EU) service or through shipping from your local warehouse.

Step by Step Guide

Setting up a seller account

In order to start selling on Amazon, the first requirement is to set up an Amazon Seller Central account. The process is pretty straight forward as Amazon only requires you to fill in your personal details to set up the account.

Your Seller Central account will allow you to reach millions of customers through the Amazon platform. When you register on the Amazon UK website, you will also gain access to Amazon's European marketplaces.

There are two options for registering as a seller. A basic seller account and a professional seller account. These both have different prices and fees, as displayed in the image below:

	Basic Sell a Role	Recommended plan PROFESSIONAL Sell a lot
Designed for sellers who plan on selling	Fewer than 35 items per month	More than 35 items per month
Key plan benefits	Pay only when you sell something	Best value for volume sales
Monthly Subscription Fee	None	£25 (excl. VAT)
Selling Fees	£0.75 (per item sold) + additional fees*	additional fees*
*For detailed fees reference: Seller Central Fee Schedule	basic account	Professional account

Image 1. Screenshot showing seller plans.

When first setting up your account, you should register as a basic seller so you can get familiar with the Seller Central platform. To register your seller account as a basic seller, scroll all the way down to the bottom of the page as Amazon tends to hide this option in small letters. You can use your basic seller account to create your product listing and send your inventory to Amazon. Once you're ready, you can then upgrade to a professional account.

<u>Seller Central Sign Up</u>

A professional seller account will allow you to create sponsored ads for your products, win the buy box, and create promotions. It also works out cheaper in the long run as you will be paying a fixed monthly fee instead of a fee per item sold.

Amazon fees

It is also important to consider the fees you will have to pay to Amazon before you decide on your product. The fees will be applicable for services including order fulfilment, which is the entire process from customer service to the delivery of the item to the customer by Amazon, as well as storage of the item in their warehouse, and leveraging Amazon's platform.

Amazon charges fulfilment fees based on factors such as size, weight, and destination. These fees are per item sold. However, the price range between different products can vary a lot, so it's essential to refer to Amazon's FBA fees pricing tab for the exact price for your product.

<u>Amazon FBA Fees</u>

Storage fees are charged monthly based on the amount of space in cubic feet you use in the Amazon warehouse. The fees are varied depending on whether you are storing items during the low season (January to September) or the high season (October to December). The exact information for this is also in the link above.

Referral fees are fees charged by Amazon for leveraging their platform. Amazon sets a different percentage depending on which category your product sells in. The costs tend to range from 7% to 15%. The fees apply for each item sold, and percentages are calculated based on the total sale price.

To see the exact fees that apply, click on the link below:

Referral Fees Prices

Something to bear in mind is that Amazon charges 20% VAT on top of each fee that they charge you. For example, if a fee is £1.00 for fulfilling an item, Amazon will deduct £1.20, having the 20 pence account for VAT. I would suggest remembering to include this when doing your calculations.

Finding your first product

Looking for your first product can be a daunting experience, especially when you are new to selling online. So, where do you begin? Do you start by searching for items that you own at home and source those? NO! Matter fact, HELL NO! As you may know, the internet is an ever-growing platform; every day, different products are created and sold online that we may not have heard of previously.

Luckily this means you won't have to reinvent the wheel to make some sales. All you will be doing is a little digging to find an item that meets your product criteria.

The following are the key factors to consider when searching for a potential product:

- **Existing product demand** - You want to find a product that is already selling online. Ideally, the top 10 sellers for the product (excluding sponsored ads that would appear at the top of the list) should sell around 1500-2000 units in total per month.
  - Low seasonality is also ideal, meaning the item sells all year round and is not one that only sells during a particular season (e.g. a product related to Christmas).
- **Low competition** - You want to ensure that you can easily get into the market. Again, you'll be able to analyse this by checking the top 10 sellers for the product (excluding sponsored ads). We want at least three of the sellers to have less than 30 reviews so that we can easily catch up.
  - A product that can be improved can be used to your advantage, as you can make the amendments to your item and then make it stand out.

- **Good margins** - You want to find a product that sells within the price range of £10 - £40. The higher you go within this range, the more profit you'll be likely to make.
  - However, it's worthwhile to keep in mind the cost of your product. Usually, the more it sells for, the more it costs.
- **Weight/Size** - You would ideally want to reduce the cost of shipping your item both to and from the UK by ensuring it is small and lightweight.
  - This is not essential; however, reducing the shipping costs can help you to increase your profits. For a small product, you can think about whether it easily fits into a letterbox or if it can be shipped as a small/medium parcel.
- **No legal issues -** Finally, you want to make sure there are no patents or any other legal issues that may arise when selling the product you wish to sell. Usually, when only one seller is selling the product, it is worth checking for patents.

Product research software

Below are the suggested leading software to utilise during your product research. In the case study after this chapter, we will go through a real-life scenario using the criteria and the tools below to find a product.

- Helium 10 - Helium 10 offers a group of web apps and chrome extensions which are helpful while building your

21

Amazon business. You can search for products, keywords, track profits, etc. using Helium 10.

- o Helium 10 offers a free version you can use with certain limits. However, you can create your custom monthly plan or purchase an individual one starting from *$97 per month (around £75 per month)*.
- o I will mainly be using **Black Box** from the Helium 10 web app for the product research in the case study and **Xray** for further product analysis.
- o Black Box is a product research tool that searches for products you can sell on Amazon based on the criteria you provide.
- o Xray gives you a display of products, sales, reviews, and competition, which can be insightful and vital during your product research.
  Download Xray from Chrome Store

- ▢ Jungle Scout - Jungle Scout offers a product research tool as a web app and has a product analysis tool as a Chrome Extension, both included in the membership. Jungle Scout is similar to Helium 10; however, they both provide unique services such as Jungle Scout promotions, which is helpful for getting your initial sales.
  - o Jungle Scout offers its basic plan from *$39 per month (around £30 per month)*.
  - o Its feature I use most is the promotion feature, which is under the suite plan and costs *$69 per month (around £55 per month)*. If you wish, you can purchase this for one month and then cancel after.

Case study: Finding a product

Image 2. Showing product research criteria put into Black Box (Helium10 product finder)

Image 3. Analysing baby shower decorations products using Jungle Scout's Chrome Extension

23

In *Image 2*, I've used the Black Box tool from Helium10. Referring to the image, you can see the criteria from the previous section inserted into Black Box. This resulted in a list of products where I then chose the baby shower decorations, shown in *Image 3*.

Image 3 shows the use of Jungle Scout's Chrome Extension. It displays a thorough analysis of the baby shower decoration with the price, revenue, reviews, etc. This feature is also accessible using Xray from Helium 10; however, I used Jungle Scout because you can simply remove all the sponsored products.

For shortlisting products from Black Box, I like to focus on finding products that meet all the criteria mentioned and are easy to manufacture to avoid customer complications with the items (for example, electricals that may stop functioning). Durable products are desirable as they will go through a lot of handling, shipping, etc.

Since we want a product that has the top 10 items selling about 1500 units, I picked a range of 200-400 unit sales per month. This would show results for 1 product, and you can then assume the competitors will make up for the other 1000+ units in sales. You want to make sure the distribution of sales is even and that there isn't one seller or brand which dominates the market.

For reviews, I would suggest entering around 25 reviews (maximum of 30) or less in Black Box. The reason for this is so you can easily compete with other sellers in your market after launching your product.

In *Image 3*, you can see I've now found a potential product; this product is a baby shower decoration kit. By looking at the data, you can already see that there's a high volume of sales for this product. There is one seller who does a huge velocity of sales, whereas the others sell a few hundred units. Also, we can see that some sellers barely have any reviews, however somehow, they still managed to gain a few hundred unit sales as well.

From these facts, you can tell that a new seller can come into the market with low reviews and still be able to make 200-400 sales in a month, with an estimated profit of £5 per item.

$$300 \; units \; sold \; per \; month \times £5 \; profit \; per \; unit = £1,500 \; total \; profit \; per \; month$$

These will be good margins to aim for, particularly when you first begin. However, don't be disappointed if you don't hit these targets as you can always improve when you launch your next products.

As a bonus, I've attached an Excel document which you can use to keep track of the products you find. (This is a view-only document so you'll have to click 'File' >> 'Download' in order to edit it).

Product Research Sheet

Sourcing from suppliers

China has become a powerhouse for our current economy, and its impact is visible all around us. With a rapid rise in productivity growth and large access to capital in the form of domestic savings and foreign investment, it's unsurprising that a majority of products sold globally come from China.

With this rapid rise to the economy, we've got entrepreneurs like Jack Ma, founder of Alibaba thinking big and making it easier for sellers/buyers all around the world to connect with manufacturers in China through the platform Alibaba.

I know some of you may be concerned about sending your money to someone on the other side of the world, whom you probably have never met. It's a perfectly reasonable concern, especially if this is your first time; however, this chapter will go through the process of finding a reliable and honest supplier for your product using the supplier criteria sheet below. (This is a view-only document so you'll have to go to 'File' >> 'Download' in order to edit it).

Supplier Sheet

I'd recommend using Alibaba for sourcing your item. The reason for this is that Alibaba has a vast range of manufacturers who are rated by their response rate, transaction-level, and the length of time they've been active on the platform. The suggested guidelines for selecting a great supplier are to make sure:

- They have been on the platform for at least three years.
- They have a response rate of over 90%.
- The seller supports Trade Assurance: A free service that protects your orders from payment to delivery.

I'd recommend finding at least five different suppliers for the product you want and contacting all of them. It's advisable to ask for the following:

- Their MOQ (Minimum order quantity)
  - I'd recommend starting small when launching a new product in case of any errors. This could be an order of about 100 units.
- Price for the number of units you want.
- Price of a product sample.
- Whether they offer DDP (Delivered duty paid)- meaning that the supplier assumes all costs associated with transporting the item to you, such as customs duties and taxes.

It is worth noting that the prices of the samples do run slightly higher than the individual cost for the product. Also, I would suggest getting a sample from at least two different suppliers to compare the quality of the products.

Once you've got all the information from the suppliers, it's time to compare them in the supplier sheet provided above and figure out which supplier will be best for you to choose. I would say the most important things to look for in a supplier are good prices to stay competitive, as well as excellent and fast communication for when you eventually need some assistance further down the line.

Creating a product listing

Now that you've found a supplier for your product, examined your sample, and you are ready to go ahead with your order, it's time to work on your product listing while you wait for the arrival of your stock.

When launching a product on FBA, I'd strongly suggest private labelling, which is essentially creating a brand/customising a pre-existing product. Therefore, while others will have a similar product to you, no one on Amazon will have your exact product with your branding.

When people hear the term brand, they think of a fancy label, beautiful packaging, and a nice colourful logo. However, this isn't the case on Amazon. To create your own brand, all you have to do is make sure the name you decide on isn't a registered trademark, since we don't want to come across any lawsuits. You can check for existing trademarks by visiting the GOV.UK website and searching the trademark registry.

Since you will be launching a new product, there are some requirements you will need to fulfil in order to get your listing set up. The first hoop to jump through is to get a UPC (Universal Product Code), these are the basic barcodes scanned whenever you buy a product. They are inexpensive and easy to purchase. I purchase mine from https://ezupc.com/buy/, and I have had no issues thus far. However, if you wish, you can buy your barcodes elsewhere.

To set up your product listing go to Seller Central >> 'Log In' >> click 'Catalogue' on the main bar of the *homepage* >> select 'Add Product' from the options >> select 'I'm Adding a Product Not Sold on Amazon'. You'll then have to choose the category your product will be in, the best way to do this is to find the best seller for your product and 'permanently borrow' a few details from them. Let's call it inspiration.

The next step will be to fill in all the details as requested by Amazon as accurately as you can. To create the perfect listing, however, we'll have to dig a little deeper than just finding a product and getting the UPC. This leads us to our next topic, keyword research.

Keyword research

Keywords are a crucial component in having customers being able to find your product and getting those first few sales. There are a few ways you can complete your keyword research, the easiest of them being the use of Cerebro by Helium 10. Cerebro displays to you the keywords your competitors are using. To do this, simply type in their product ASINs (found on Amazon on the product page under product information just below additional information) into Cerebro's intuitive platform to uncover what keywords they're using in their listing. You can then use these keywords for your listing as well.

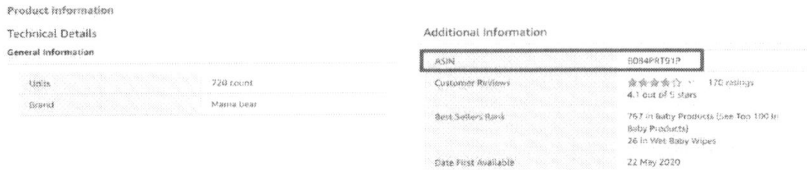

Image 4. Product ASIN location on the product page.

Copying your competitors' keywords is an effective way of finding out what already works; however, tools such as www.keywordtool.io can also be beneficial by helping you find additional keywords for free.

You can also find out which terms customers type in most on Amazon by using the search bar. To do this, type in the main keyword for your product. For example, if you type in 'foam roller', Amazon will suggest popular keywords in the form of a drop-down that customers tend to search for when searching for foam rollers. (*See Image 4*).

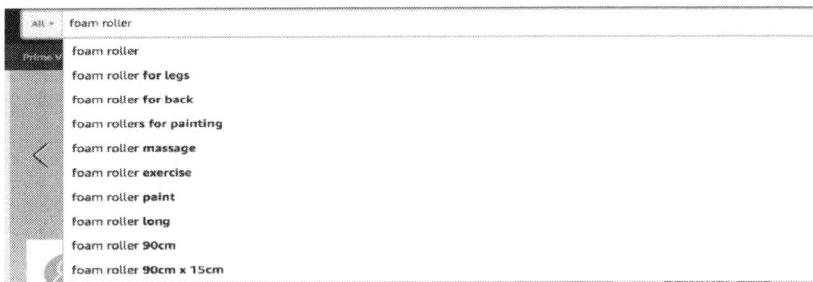

Image 5. Dropdown menu of 'foam roller' most popular keywords.

When you've got your list of keywords most frequently used by your customers, you can then create your title, as well as include your key product features, and product description which should integrate all if not a majority of your most popular keywords.

The title is the main part of your listing customers will use to identify your product, along with the product image. To make sure it's easily recognisable as to what your product is, make sure the first 80 characters clearly state what your product is and what differentiates it from your competitors.

Product images

Apart from your title, the images are said to be the most crucial part of your product listing. Since your customers won't be able to touch your product and experience it, you'll have to do your best to convey what benefits the customers will get by choosing to purchase your product.
Amazon does have a few guidelines when it comes to uploading product pictures; these are the following:

- Images must accurately represent the product and only show the product that is for sale.
- The product and all its features must be visible.
- The main image should have a pure white background.

- The main images must be professional photographs of the actual product (graphics, illustrations, mock-ups, or placeholders are not allowed). They must not show excluded accessories; props that might confuse the customer; text that is not part of the product; or logos, watermarks, or inset images.
- Images must match the product title.
- Images should be 1,000 pixels or larger in either height or width. This minimum size requirement enables the zoom function on the website, which has proved to enhance sales. The smallest that your file can be is 500 pixels on its longest side.
- Images must not exceed 10,000 pixels on the longest side.
- Amazon accepts JPEG (.jpg), TIFF (.tif) or GIF (.gif) file formats, but JPEG is preferred.
- Their servers do not support animated GIFs.

The guidelines are pretty straight forward; I'd say the main point to watch out for is the white background for the first/main image. If you are using a professional photography service, make sure they have previous experience of taking pictures of Amazon products.

However, if you want to save some money, you can decide to take the pictures yourself, simply make sure you get yourself a product photography toolkit on eBay. This will provide you with essential things such as lighting and a white background. You can also use Fiverr to have your pictures edited or to add the white background.

When exploring what sort of ideas to capture for your product pictures, it's always a good idea to have a look at the images created by your competitors who sell a similar item to your product as well as those who sell a similar item in other marketplaces. I would suggest including infographics and a few lifestyle pictures. Amazon allows up to seven images for most products; however, this can vary based on the product category.

Sending inventory into Amazon

Now that the essentials are out the way for creating a listing, you can finally set up your first shipment to the Amazon warehouse.

To set up a shipment, you need to go to your inventory page and click the drop-down menu on the right-hand side of the product that you want to send inventory for, and select 'Send/Replenish Inventory'. (*See Image 5).*

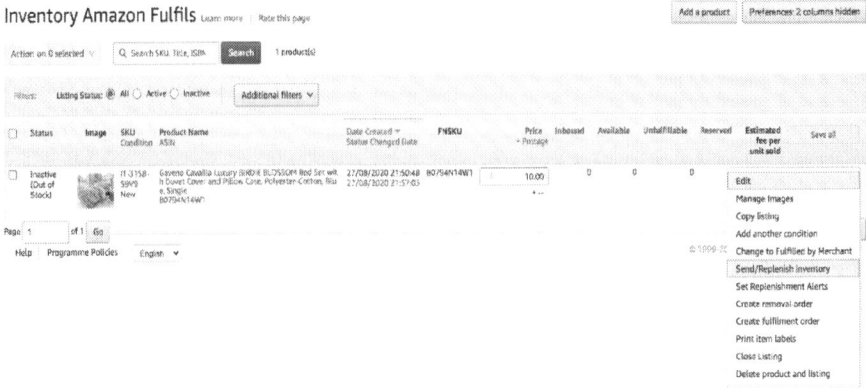

Image 6. Sending inventory to Amazon

You will need to start by creating a new shipping plan and select the ship from-address that can be either the supplier's address or your own address. You then have to state how your products will be packed; this can be either as individual products packed together in one box or case packed items, which essentially means each box contains the same items.

Since we will most likely be shipping the products from the supplier to the warehouse, they will be case packed, which means you'll have to declare the units per case, as well as the number of cases. For example, let's say we're sending 200 pens packed into four boxes, each box containing 50 pens meaning we'd have four boxes in total.

Units per case = 50
Number of cases = 4

The next step is to check if the items you are sending into Amazon requires any preparation in order to meet Amazon's prep guidelines. These are requirements such as putting fragile labels on items that are easily breakable (e.g. glass) or putting suffocation labels on items wrapped in plastic. You should have a chat with your supplier, and they should be able to sort these out for you. However, if they aren't able to do this, Amazon can also prep your items for you for a small fee per unit.

Amazon will then provide you with a code known as FNSKU, which is a unique barcode required for all FBA stock. Your supplier will need to put these on each individual unit in order for Amazon to scan them in and add them to your stock count. As stated previously, Amazon can label your products for you for a small fee.

You should now have a ship-to address, and Amazon will usually receive a shipment from your supplier as long as there aren't any unpaid fees due at arrival. This shouldn't be an issue if you have a delivery agreement, such as DDP.

It's recommended to ship a small number of units (100-200) for your first shipment. This is to test the market and minimise risk. Therefore, you should pick small parcel delivery as the delivery method and select your carrier from the options provided.

Finally, Amazon will request the packing information for your shipment in order to provide you with labels for the boxes. **Each box will have its own individual label**, make sure your supplier knows this and doesn't use one label for all the boxes.

The packing information you will need for your labels is the units per box, the number of boxes, weight, and dimension.

You can now print off your box labels and send them to your supplier.

Ranking on the first page

If you've followed all the steps this far, then you should have completed your listing, which includes your primary keywords and impressive images to attract your customers as well as inventory ready to ship out.

Most sales on Amazon come from the first page; an estimated 75% of internet users don't scroll past the first page. Therefore, we'll do everything in our power to make sure our product gets on the first page. The higher up on the first page, the better. There are a few methods used to accomplish this goal.

Running sponsored ads: This is the most common approach used by sellers and is beneficial when you've done your keywords research thoroughly. There are two campaign types you can perform, which are:
- Sponsored products: These are focused on individually advertising products to shoppers using related keywords or similar products.
- Sponsored brands: These are ads to showcase your product range once you've registered your brand.

You will be using the sponsored product campaign to boost your ranking. Since you've done your keyword research, you will be using manual targeting (your own keywords/ similar products) instead of automatic targeting (Amazon's suggestions for your keywords).

Before you activate your campaign, you need to set a daily budget you want to spend. Since there is no specific formula for making ads work, you'll have to experiment to see what works best for you. Therefore, a daily budget of about £5 is recommended to start with and scaling up or down depending on how well your campaign does.

Since you're launching your product, you want to be aggressive with your keywords initially. Therefore, when you enter your main keywords, you want to set your bidding strategy to dynamic bids. Dynamic bids allow Amazon to raise and decrease your bid depending on if it's likely to convert to a sale or not.

I recommend creating two campaigns, one that targets keywords and one that targets similar products.
Let's start by creating the keyword-targeted campaign. There are three match types you can use for your keywords:
- Broad match: Contains all the keywords in any order with plurals, variation, and related keywords.
- Phrase match: Contains the exact phrase or sequence of keywords.
- Exact match: Exactly matches the keyword or sequence of words.

For all your keywords, you want to use and experiment with all three match types to decide, which brings you the best result for the best price. You can easily analyse this by checking the ACOS (Advertising Cost of Sale). ACOS is a metric used to measure the performance of an Amazon sponsored product campaign and indicates the amount spent in order to get a sale. You want to keep all your keywords that have a low ACOS and are profitable. However, it isn't uncommon to lose money while ranking as you will make it back after your product is high up on the first page.

Each keyword and match type that correlates with it will have individual prices suggested by Amazon. These are usually valuable suggestions; however, to get on the first page, test the suggested price with an increase of 10-20%. Launch your campaign, and within 15 minutes, check where Amazon has decided to place your ad by searching for your keyword and adjust accordingly.

Targeting products is a more straightforward and newer way to advertise on Amazon. When you do this, you'll notice that your ads will show up on the targeted products' page. This allows you to organically gain a spot under *'Customers who viewed this item also viewed'* which is a valuable piece of real estate to own as Amazon does the advertising for you.

To create a targeted product ad, you follow the same procedure to create a keyword-targeted ad; however, when you pick your targeting option, you click 'Product targeting' instead.

You can then choose to target your product category, specific products, or a brand. Amazon will suggest a category for you and a bunch of products. However, you can also find products manually by finding their ASIN, which, as you know, can be found under the product information on the product page.

As with all ads, you will have to test which products give you the best return on investment and adjust your marketing campaign accordingly.

Jungle Scout promotions is a web app which can be beneficial when first launching your product. The web app plugs you into a vast pool of buyers that want to buy products at a discounted price. We refer to services like this as giveaway services. This tool can improve your products ranking, get you reviews and accelerate your sales. The only downside of using giveaways to rank your product is that customers usually want a discount of more than 50%. However, I have used these services and have found the return on investment worthwhile.

Getting reviews for your product

Reviews are a vital part of selling any product or service online. Reviews help your customers decide on your offer, prove whether you are credible or trustworthy, and help you gain visibility in an otherwise crowded marketplace.

No one wants to be the first person to buy a product without any reviews. Customers need to be incentivised by low prices/high discounts in order for the rewards to outweigh the risks. Therefore, you want to focus on getting at least five reviews for your product.

Amazon automatically sends out an email to each customer (provided they haven't opted out) to review your product and seller account after each purchase. They also allow you to request a customer review manually when you view the order details on Seller Central. You can automate this process by using software explicitly created for increasing reviews:

List of 7 best software

You can also be proactive and use this software to send out follow-up emails to each customer. You can provide excellent customer service, ask them to kindly leave you a review and also offer them a discount. Offering customers discounts to leave a review is against Amazon's policy; however, you can give them a discount code irrespective of whether they leave you a review or not. Also, make it a key point for them to leave you an honest review and not a positive or a 5-star review. Depending on your risk affinity, you could also incentivise potential customers online to buy your product in exchange for a discount or a free product.

You can also do this by asking your friends to leave you a review as long as you aren't tightly connected to them, as Amazon sometimes tends to delete reviews from people that they believe are closely related to you. For example, work colleagues or family members that you are always around.

Another method to gain reviews is to have your suppliers put a product insert into your packaging. With this insert, you can put helpful information about your product, your website/social media, and finally, ask your customers to leave you a review.

You can incentivise customers to follow you on social media or go to your website, so have a handy e-book or discount code ready for your customers to use.

Expanding sales to EU marketplaces

Amazon offers a seamless experience for both the customers and the sellers; therefore, it comes to no surprise selling in EU marketplaces is made as simple as can be.

There are two different ways which you can use to ship your products to the EU marketplaces, which as of now include: Germany, Spain, Italy, France & Netherlands.

The first method is when you ship through the EFN (European Fulfilment Network). This is the quickest way to set up your listings for selling in Europe; however, this method will cost you more.

Products fulfilled through the EFN are stored in the European country where your business is registered and then shipped out to customers in Europe when ordered. Shipping products through EFN can help you get a sense of what countries are likely to order your products and which countries to focus your growth on more.

Shipping products across borders, however, does take time, which means that your products won't be eligible for prime shipping. The cost of shipping products across borders also tends to be higher than the alternative method, which is Pan European FBA.

With Pan European FBA, your inventory is stored in different countries across Europe. This allows you to be eligible for the prime badge for your listings and also enjoy local shipping rates for your products.

There are some measures you have to put in place to be eligible for Pan European FBA; these are legal requirements in order to store your products in different countries. You have to be VAT registered in all Pan European countries to take advantage of this service. This can cost around €3000 to set up; however, Amazon usually has a promotion for which they allow you to register and get your VAT filings done for a year for free.

VAT services on Amazon

Bonus

What to do when you run out of stock

Once in a while, every seller runs out of stock, which is a problem, but a good problem. It means you've got a product that is high in demand, which is always a plus. To minimise the loss of sales during this period, I've got a little trick for you, which I use myself when this happens.

What we're going to do is change our product from fulfilled by Amazon to fulfilled by merchant (FBM), which can be edited by clicking the drop-down menu next to the product on the inventory page. The next step is to select, 'Edit', and change the 'In-Stock Date' (under the 'Offer' tab) to a week or two after you expect your shipment to arrive. This is in case there are any delays; we don't want any disappointed customers.

Building a brand

Finding products that are in high demand is an excellent idea and a good business model to generate a substantial amount of money. However, if you could do better, should you? Of course!

Therefore, looking into creating a brand around your products is an idea to consider. The reason being when you create a brand, you have the ability to build an audience, people who support your brand and recognise the standard and integrity of your products. This will give you the opportunity to launch new products effortlessly since you already have the audience for it.

Selling replenishable stock

When you look at the products that Amazon creates and sells, you notice a high affinity for products like diapers, toilet paper, and baby wipes. These are products where they know they can gain repeat customers. The same goes for brands like Primark, Coca-Cola, and McDonalds; they create a system that makes it easy for you to come back.

Keeping account of sales

There are a few software which can help you keep account of sales for your Amazon business. Currently, I have been using Fetcher which is offered by Jungle Scout.

I have been in contact with a few sellers online and have noticed a majority of sellers use Xero in conjunction with Link My Books which work together on the Xero's platform. I'm yet to try this out and will update the book accordingly.

Joining a community

As sellers we're not always going to have all the answers, we're going to have a few moments when we don't know what to do, or we need someone to give us a helping hand. In moments like these, I find it helpful to be able to post in groups dedicated to Amazon FBA on Facebook. However, you can also send an email to us at jaxs-education@outlook.com.

Amazon FBA sellers checklist

As a final parting gift for you to help you get through your journey, here is a checklist you can use to stay on track till you launch your first product:

Amazon FBA Checklist

What now?

Epilogue

Congratulations on the completion of this book, you are a star! Only 10% of people will reach the end of this book, and you are one of them, you now have all the information required to start a successful Amazon business.

However, this is not the end. To be making money while you sleep, you need to put in the action required. Work smart now so you can enjoy life later. Before I leave, I want to share with you this quote, which inspired me to write this book and work on earning my financial independence.

> *"If you don't find a way to make money while you sleep, you will work until you die." - Warren Buffet*

Might have not been the quote you wanted to read at the end of this book; however, this is a quote that will stand the test of time. The quicker you find a way to create passive income for yourself, the quicker you can go on and live the life you deserve.

I wish you the best on your journey and lots of success in all your endeavours.

Stay hungry and stay foolish.

For any queries, further information, or service, please contact
jaxs-education@outlook.com.

I will do my utmost best to respond to each email personally.

Yours sincerely,

Jason A. Kwao

Printed in Great Britain
by Amazon